PENDRAGON

THE CORONATION CHAIR IN WESTMINSTER ABBEY.

Mahmoud Shelton

Pendragon

Essays Collected for the Coronation of King Charles III

Temple of Justice Books

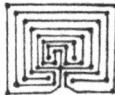

Printed in the United States of America

ISBN 978-0-9741468-6-7

Photo credits
Page 18: Abhijit Patil
Page 44: Getty Images

CONTENTS

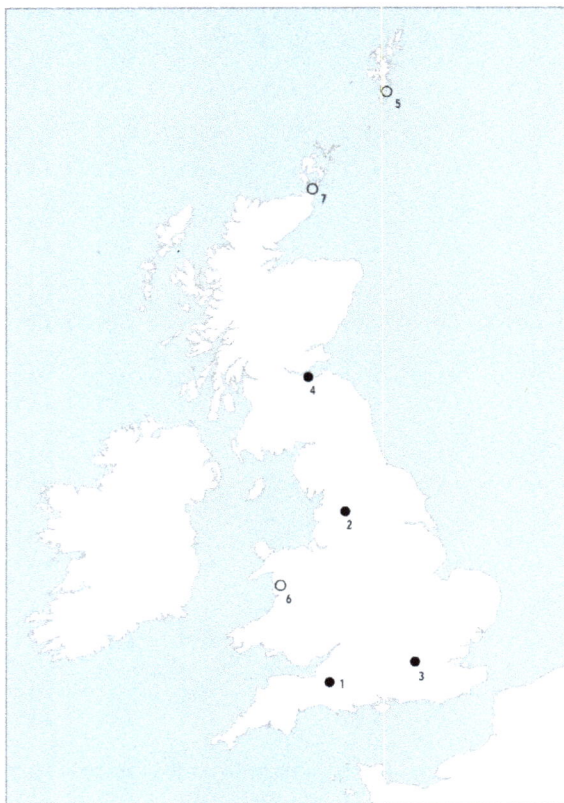

The Seven Spiritual Centers of Britain

Introduction

The writings in this collection do not all pertain immediately to the crowning of HM King Charles III. Rather they relate thematically to significant events in the British royal family's recent history, and especially the coronation; yet they are not presented here in accordance with the chronological order of those events. The essay of foremost relevance is "The Arcane Setting for the Coronation," appearing here for the first time to coincide with the ceremony so that the symbolism involved might be better understood. The other essays have been available in the past but were deemed of sufficient interest to be made available together in this volume, though some minor modifications have been necessary to account for recent developments. The following essays are also thematically related through the doctrine of the Seven Spiritual Centers of Britain, an idea first indicated by the Islamic authority Shaykh Nazim al-Haqqani in 2011 and on which

I subsequently offered a commentary in *Sacred Geography and the Paths of the Sun*.[1] A map from that volume is reproduced on page 6 to help conceptualize this idea, but this map is only provisional; some contextual notes on the role of Shaykh Nazim should be still more helpful.

Muhammad Nazim `Adil was born on 21 April 1922 in Cyprus when the island was still under British governance; his birthday would also be that of the future Queen Elizabeth II four years later. His spiritual training was primarily under the direction of the Daghestani-Naqshbandi Shaykh `Abdullah of Damascus,[2] the "Sultan of Saints." Shaykh Nazim al-Haqqani ("the True") ultimately became his successor, and made a yearly practice of spending Ramadan, the most sacred month of the Islamic calendar, in the Christian land of England. For a quarter century until 1999, Shaykh Nazim was able to meet the needs of spiritual seekers from every corner of the world, Muslim or not, in the worldly hub of London.[3] Curiously, perhaps, he attributed this

---

[1] Temple of Justice Books, 2021.

[2] Cf. *Mysteries of Dune: Sufism, Psychedelics, and the Prediction of Frank Herbert*, Temple of Justice Books, 2020.

[3] Recall the note by Michel Vâlsan concerning the supreme spiritual authority or *qutb*: "in Islamic esoterism, and according to its proper 'perspective,' it is said that the Qutb provides his providential help not

arrangement to the blessing of Britain's royal family. He was therefore always generous in his praise for HM The Queen and her son Charles, then Prince of Wales.

The heir apparent was the longest serving Prince of Wales in history, who chose to define his role by the defense of nature and tradition. In 1993, Prince Charles delivered his famous speech on "Islam and the West" at the Sheldonian Theater in Oxford. In the years that followed, Shaykh Nazim spoke approvingly of him:

> We are also happy that His Highness Crown Prince Charles is more interested in Islam than any other prince, even more than any other king's son…Even though he belongs and is nominated to be the Head of the Church of England, he says such brave and honest words about Islam…We ask Allah Almighty to give Prince Charles more honour and more power… Happy days, happy future for the whole British nation![4]

only to Muslims…" (cf. *Sacred Geography and the Paths of the Sun*, op. cit., pages 103-4).

[4] Maulana Sheik Nazim al Haqqani, *Power Oceans of Light*, London: Zero Productions, 1995, pages 61-2.

The media would ask Shaykh Nazim about the Prince's consistent defense of Islam, and in an interview with the BBC he made the following claim: "My soul is guiding his soul in the spiritual world. Even though I have not met His Highness, my soul has been his guide within the spiritual world and will continue to be so here forever."[5] With the death of Princess Diana in 1997, Shaykh Nazim warned that her tragic fate had been a consequence of her rejection of the great honor she had been given, and continued to express hope for the future king:[6] ""May Allah bless him and put a powerful crown on his head to correct every wrong thing in the United Kingdom!"[7]

Following a long life as a traditional renewer in East and West, Shaykh Nazim al-

---

[5] Sheik Nazim al Haqqani, *Secret Desires: Talks Given in 1996 in Germany and Great Britain by a Sufi Master of Our Time,* London: Zero Productions, 1996, page 108.

[6] The warnings and happy tidings of Shaykh Nazim may be compared with the prophetic mission: "Lo! We have sent thee (O Muhammad) with the truth, a bringer of glad tidings and a warner..." (*Qur`an* II, 119)

[7] Sheik Nazim al Haqqani, *Princess Diana's Death,* London: Zero Productions, 1997, page 40. As with so many of the books bearing the name of the Shaykh, this volume was compiled by his close disciple Zahra Quensel, who did so in this case with particular care and compassion. Better known as Zero, Quensel was of Swedish origin; her grave is located near Glastonbury.

Haqqani passed away in 2014. HM Queen Elizabeth II passed some eight years later, whose incomparable reign ensured the preservation of the British monarchy through the upheavals of the modern era. Now, a quarter century after Shaykh Nazim prayed for the crowning of the king, the time for his coronation has arrived.

The ceremony in Westminster Abbey obviously involves a profound symbolism, and in a sacred context, symbols have the power to unite Heaven and Earth. The map of the Seven Spiritual Centers provides another example of this, with its geographical locations mysteriously arranged like the stars of the sky. At Glastonbury (point 1 on the map), there is further evidence of stellar symbolism in the form of its landscape zodiac.[8] The Arthurian name chosen for this collection, Pendragon, likewise relates to the stars, since the luminous aspect of the dragon is best represented by the constellation Draco surrounding the Pole Star that is traditionally

---

[8] Cf. René Guénon, "The Land of the Sun," *Symbols of Sacred Science*, Hillsdale: Sophia Perennis, 2004. K.E. Maltwood who rediscovered the ancient pattern presumed that the effigies were the source of Arthurian legend rather than in some manner corresponding to it. In a similar manner, proponents of "British Israelism" have claimed that the traditions of Britain are the source of the sacred histories of the Bible, instead of properly acknowledging their correspondences.

described as being "in the middle of heaven like a king upon his throne."[9]

Traditional lore insists on the ancient presence of Jesus in Glastonbury, as well as that place's identity as the oldest Christian site in Europe, and this lore specifically informs the anthem of England that ponders "And did those feet in ancient time walk upon Englands mountains green." Now, it is important to recognize that the apocalyptic return of Jesus from the celestial realm is a doctrine belonging both to Christianity and Islam. Shaykh Nazim al-Haqqani always insisted on the approach of a Heavenly Kingdom of Jesus Christ on Earth, and that the destiny of King Charles belonged to it. At the very least, the crowning of a king in "Englands green & pleasant land" who is worthy of uniting the allegiances of Muslims as well as Christians[10] prefigures this return.

Ramadan 1444

---

[9] Quotation from the *Sepher Yetsirah* in René Guénon, "The Wild Boar and the Bear," *Symbols of Sacred Science,* op. cit. The Arabic name of the Pole Star is Qutb (see note 3 above).

[10] According to Arthurian legend, or as it was known the "Matter of Britain," King Arthur even attracted Saracens such as Sir Palamedes to his court.

Celestial Events Accompanying the Ascendancy of HM King Charles III

At the moment when the passing of HM Queen Elizabeth II was announced, rainbows appeared concurrently above the British monarch's residences in London and in Windsor, as was reported by innumerable eyewitnesses and transmitted widely through the media. The popular reaction to their appearance was to recognize them as portents, and so there were fanciful attempts to interpret them accordingly. The rainbow is of course a symbol, and as such is well-known from the Book of Genesis. Not surprisingly, it has also been employed in anti-traditional contexts, especially in recent years; but in the case of its recent use in Britain as a sign of hope during the COVID-19 crisis, it could be

Rainbow over Windsor Castle on 8 September 2022

maintained that in some measure this meaning derives from its traditional significance in the Christian world, of which Britain has long been in a position of leadership. According to the Bible, the rainbow is "the sign of the covenant" between the Divine and the human, and no doubt hope depends upon this covenant; but as for the timing of this sign's appearance that marked the passing of a monarch, no doubt its significance relates especially to the matter of succession, since the latter is above all an affirmation of a covenant expressed through the Divine Right of Kings. Just as these rainbows were seen to be portents, we should not overlook some of the other celestial events that have appeared as we await the coronation of the King on 6 May.

In the days between his accession and the funeral of his predecessor, HM King Charles III undertook what amounted to a ceremonial tour of Great Britain. On 14 September, the day after the royal visit to Northern Ireland, a spectacular fireball streaked across British skies during the midevening, that is, at a time for all to see. Sightings were everywhere reported from Scotland to London, and consistently described

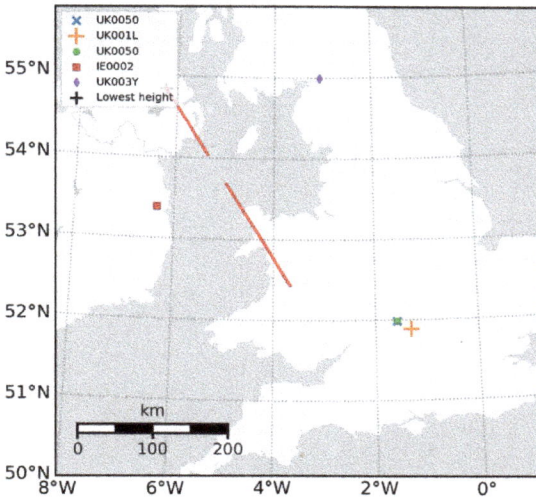

Path of the fireball on 14 September 2002 according to the UK Meteor Network

the distinctly green appearance of the meteor. Scientists were able to plot the trajectory of the celestial event, and its path was remarkable indeed, though none seemed to note a coincidence. The fireball was apparently in line with the very place HM The King had visited the day before. Moreover, all four of the "Devolved Nations" were visited personally by the monarch during that week, and midway through that same week (i.e. Wednesday) the meteor became a unifying experience for the people of those same nations. No doubt this event was as timely and meaningful as the rainbows, but to approach an understanding of what the fireball signifies, we must turn to an account of another ruler's accession in Geoffrey of Monmouth's *History of the Kings of Britain*.

That ruler was Uther Pendragon, and Geoffrey describes a celestial portent on the passing of Uther's predecessor that became the source of the name "Pendragon:" "there appeared a star of wonderful magnitude and brightness, darting forth a ray, at the end of which was a globe of fire in form of a dragon…" Merlin informs Uther of the proper interpretation of the event: "the star, and the fiery dragon under it, signifies yourself," and Merlin extends the particulars of its multiple-rayed appearance to Uther's descendants, especially his "most potent son" Arthur. Because of this interpretation, the dragon becomes the emblem of Uther and so also of his rightful heirs, and the dragon of Wales supposedly derives from it. "Pendragon" is therefore a title, and indeed King Arthur was also known as Pendragon during the Victorian Age. The insight of a wizard is hardly required to see the connection between the tour of the new king and the appearance of the fiery meteor; and one is left to conclude that Pendragon is an especially suitable title for HM Charles III, who is also, lest it be overlooked, named Arthur.

However, it is possible that the Medieval event described by Geoffrey was in actuality a comet rather than a meteor. Yet during the days midway between the accession of HM The King and his scheduled coronation, the skies were also visited by a comet known by the rather uninspired name of "C/2022 E3 (ZTF)." Though barely visible to the naked eye, this comet passed from a position in the constellation Corona Borealis towards the constellation Taurus. Now, the relevance of a Corona Borealis or "Northern Crown" to the coronation of a British monarch is obvious enough, and it is no less relevant that 6 May belongs to the zodiacal house of Taurus. Very remarkably, sky watchers observed that the comet was, like the fireball, of a distinctly green color; and rather like the fireball of Geoffrey, this comet was strangely triple-rayed. Its path included the constellation Draco, or Dragon, and passed between Ursa Major and Ursa Minor, the Great and Little Bears.

Above all, the presence of this green comet among these stars concerns the "green &

17

pleasant land" above all others. These constellations are circumpolar and visible to the north, of course, just as Britain is positioned in the north. It is also well known that the name Arthur means "bear," and Ursa Major was in former times called Arthur's Wain, or "chariot." Even more remarkably, the joining of the names "Arthur" and "Pendragon" recalls the proximity of the bear constellations to Draco. In remote antiquity, according to René Guénon, the bear constellations were instead identified with the Balance or Scales, before this name was shifted to the zodiac; but even this identification is significant here, since Gildas in the 6th century describes Britain specifically as being "poised in the divine balance." In *Sacred Geography and the*

Paths of the Sun,[11] I explored how this astral symbolism helps confirm the locations of the Seven Spiritual Centers of Britain, since not all were precisely indicated when the spiritual master Shaykh Nazim al-Haqqani revealed their existence.

As for the other celestial portents under consideration, they may be shown to have manifested in relation to certain of these spiritual centers. Windsor that witnessed the rainbow of 8 September is indicated by point 3 on the map on page 6. Concerning the fireball, if we compare its trajectory to the map of spiritual centers, it will be observed that the meteor passed *precisely* over point 6 that marks the mountain of Cader Idris, or "Seat of Idris." These observations may be taken further. Indicated by point 4 on the map, Edinburgh became center stage ahead of London for the ceremonial role of HM The King in the mortuary observances for his mother, which included a chivalric vigil. Another coincidence relating to the Seven Spiritual Centers occurred more recently, with the monarch visiting Greater Manchester on 20 January 2023, the very day that the son and apparent successor of Shaykh Nazim, on a special tour of England from his home in Istanbul, was visiting the center marked 2 on the map in the same region.

---

[11] Op. cit., chapter 8.

In an article on the symbolism of the rainbow,[12] René Guénon emphasizes the association between the rainbow and the serpent, and he provides examples of the "celestial serpent" from several traditions and mentions Goethe's story of the "green snake" in this context. Attached to recent celestial events, then, there is a clear consistency of symbolism to be observed, since the celestial serpent and dragon are essentially interchangeable, and we have noted the distinctly green appearance of both fireball and comet. Guénon's study reminds us of the luminous aspect of the serpent, which is especially valuable since the western world has long failed to perceive anything other than its dark aspect. Other symbols such as the swastika and pentagram have been similarly unbalanced in their characterization. In the case of the serpent's complex symbolism, this imbalance is despite the continued use of the Staff of Asclepios in medicine and the injunction in the Gospels to be "as wise as serpents." Even so, the luminous example of "Pendragon" is rather exceptional in the West, even though the identification of a true king with a celestial serpent or dragon is of central importance in the East.[13]

---

[12] "The Bridge and the Rainbow," *Symbols of Sacred Science,* op. cit.

[13] Just as the prefix "pen-" relates to the number 5, the dragon emblem of the Oriental emperor has five toes instead of four.

Guénon insists that the rainbow, and therefore also the celestial serpent that is its symbolic equivalent, is properly understood as the "expression of the action and reaction of forces emanating respectively from heaven and earth." In terms of the yearly cycle and its seasonal festivals, the Celts of ancient Britain seem to have preferred the cross-quarter day of early May to celebrate the marriage of these forces. It is not by accident that 6 May has been arranged as the date for HM The King's coronation, and I have already observed the relevance of that date for England and its patron saint in *Sacred Geography and the Paths of the Sun.*[14] Of course, the iconography of Saint George and the Dragon is perhaps the most explicit depiction in the Christian tradition of this "action and reaction of forces emanating respectively from heaven and earth;" yet in this case, the dragon is not celestial but terrestrial, with the heavenly aspect represented by the saint. At the same time, however, the name of this saint means "farmer," a name relating especially to earth, and so the action and reaction of forces here involves an exchange of attributes "which in such a case can be qualified quite properly as 'hierogamic.'" Saint George is known in the Islamic tradition as al-Khidr, a name that simply means "the Green," although the dragon iconography is more or less

---

[14] Op. cit., pages 113-4.

absent; yet surely this is because, to again use the words of René Guénon, he is understood to be "reintegrated into the state and the nature of 'primordial man,'"[15] and 6 May is the day of his festival.

The new "Pendragon King" is also named George. The symbolic participation of the celestial serpent in his ascendancy signals a return to the primordial harmony between the heavenly and earthly. As we have seen, this return is intimately bound up with the sacred geography of the Seven Spiritual Centers. Many years ago the future king expressed his commitment to be a defender of faith, and he has remained true to that heavenly calling. Now his role as an environmental champion, or rather as a "Defender of Nature," appears reflected in the greenness of celestial portents. Indeed, these heavenly signs seem to confirm a promise made by HM The Queen less than a year before her passing, that the defense of the Earth would ever after be a special distinction of the House of Windsor.[16]

---

[15] *The Great Triad*, Hillsdale: Sophia Perennis, 2001, page 97. On the primordial condition and the symbolism of the dragon, see "Shai-hulud" in *Mysteries of Dune*, op. cit.
[16] Address to the climate conference in Scotland, November 2021

The Arcane Setting
for the Coronation

In accordance with royal custom,
Westminster Abbey in London was chosen for
the coronation of HM King Charles III. The
Abbey is properly a church and an abbey no
longer, and while this change may be traced to
the campaign of Henry VIII against the sacred
sanctuaries of Britain, Westminster was largely
spared the ravages inflicted by this religious
reformer. Its formal designation is the Collegiate
Church of Saint Peter at Westminster, and there
is evidence that it occupies the site of a former
temple of Apollo; among other things, this
evidence suggests that the site was where the
legendary King Bladud fell following his magical
flight.[17] Many kings have since been interred at

---

[17] In the 18th century, Bath architect John Wood
identified King Bladud with Abaris the Hyperborean,
at least in part because the latter was also remembered

the site, and the center of the church has long
been dedicated to the shrine and sanctuary of the
saint and king Edward the Confessor.

At the center of the sanctuary is a
Medieval treasure in the form of its Cosmati
Pavement, and it is upon this floor that the
coronation of the monarch is traditionally
performed. The name "Cosmati" refers to a
family of Italian craftsmen renowned for the type
of geometric mosaic work represented upon the
floor at Westminster. Such mosaics are
comprised of small triangles and rectangles of
glass and colored stones which were often
incorporated from ancient monuments. As part
of his Gothic renewal of Westminster, King
Henry III brought Italian craftsmen to England
especially for this work, and the pavement's
position within the floorplan indicates that the
king intended for it to be the setting for royal
ceremony. Nevertheless, this intricate
masterpiece has rarely been seen in modern
times, and has even been covered during
previous coronations, including that of HM

---

for his supernatural flight. Abaris was of course a
follower of Apollo, and King Bladud's legendary
discovery of the mineral springs in Bath is in
accordance with Apollonian tradition (on Apollo and
mineral springs, see *Paths of the Western Sun* volume I).
Even before Wood's time, however, Shakespeare has
King Lear swear by Apollo, when King Leir is
legendarily the son of King Bladud.

Queen Elizabeth II. In a study attempting to evaluate the pavement's meaning, art historian Richard Foster ends up posing the question, "did hiding it from public view mean that its significance was too great to be an open secret?"[18]

Following a thorough conservation effort and its rededication in 2010, the Sanctuary Pavement has providentially been prepared for the coronation of the new king, and this coincidence is reason enough to reconsider its significance. What is more, it has also been dubbed the "End of the World Pavement," suggesting that its purpose is not yet fulfilled. This name in fact refers to an inscription within the pattern that, although surviving incomplete, has nevertheless been successfully deciphered:

> In the year of Christ, the thousandth, twice hundredth, twelfth, with the sixtieth, with four subtracted,[19] the third King Henry, [the Pope in] the city [of Rome], Odoric, and the Abbot [of Westminster] fixed together these porphyry stones.

---

[18] Richard Foster, *Patterns of Thought: The Hidden Meaning of the Great Pavement of Westminster Abbey*, London: Jonathan Cape, 1991, page 164.

[19] The date of the pavement is therefore 1268.

> If the reader would revolve
> prudently all the arranged
> things here he will find the end
> of the Prime Mover. Should you
> add hedges three times, dogs
> and horses and men, stags and
> ravens, eagles, tremendous sea
> monsters, the world, each thing
> following triples the years of the
> one going before.
>
> The spherical globe here shows
> the archetypal macrocosm.[20]

In the most general terms, the pattern of the mosaic is composed of circles and squares, and inasmuch as these shapes symbolize Heaven and Earth, the design is appropriate for the shrine of the saintly King Edward. More specifically, the

---

[20] Translation by David Howlett in "The Inscriptions in the Sanctuary Pavement at Westminster" (*Westminster Abbey: The Cosmati Pavements*, edited by Lindy Grant and Richard Mortimer, Abingdon-on-Thames: Routledge, 2002). Howlett subjects the words of the inscription to an analysis based upon complicated Biblical numerology, and notes that the word "end" here signifies not only chronological "conclusion" but also "purpose." The inscription's middle section has been traced to the Greek poet Hesiod (cf. Foster, op. cit., pages 102-3); its reckoning of some 19000 years likely relates less to chronology than to the symbolism of numbers, and therefore its "purpose."

The Sanctuary Pavement at Westminster

composition is dominated by formulations of the
numbers 5 and 6. The number 6 appears clearly
in the hexagrams and hexagons that recur
throughout the pattern. As for the number 5, it is
emphasized through an artistic motif called
"guilloche" that involves sinuous interweaving.
At the middle of the arrangement, the central
circle is bound by guilloche to four others at the
cardinal directions, and these five circles are

isolated within a square. This one square in turn is bound by guilloche to four more circles, one at the center of each side, and 1 + 4 = 5. Finally, each corner of the overall design is composed of five circles bound together by guilloche. These numbers in fact support the more general interpretation of the design, since 5 and 6 represent "Earth and Heaven in their reciprocal action and reaction."[21] No doubt Richard Foster is correct to trace the meaning of the Sanctuary Pavement to the teachings of Plato and Pythagoras on the science of number. In the Classical world, the number 5 was a signature of sorts of the Pythagoreans in the form of the pentalpha, and in the time of King Henry III the number 6 was specifically associated with the Pythagoreans "and those who follow their doctrines."[22] Foster fails to appreciate, however, that Plato and Pythagoras belong to a singular tradition, that of Apollo, and that the presence of these teachings at a site formerly dedicated to Apollo is not without significance in itself.

In Christian terms, the overall design of the Sanctuary Pavement is immediately comparable to a particular form of the *gammadion* (pictured opposite), especially since the five

---

[21] René Guénon, *The Great Triad*, Hillsdale: Sophia Perennis, 2001, page 56. Cf. also page 21 in this volume.
[22] Ibn Arabî, *Le Livre du Mîm, du Wâw et du Nûn*, presented by Charles-André Gilis, Beirut: Albouraq, 2002, page 61.

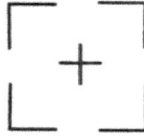

circles at the center of the Cosmati pavement are arranged in a cross. The *gammadion* is related to figural depictions of the four Evangelists around Jesus Christ, yet its geometric form encompasses related meanings comprehensible through the science of symbolism. As the foremost authority on the latter, René Guénon chooses to relate the form of the *gammadion* to the Arabic term *al-arkān*,[23] meaning 'supports." *Al-arkān* is a term applied in the Islamic tradition to the four elements of Classical cosmology - fire, air, water, and earth – while the *"rukn al-arkan"* is the fifth element or "quintessence." The relevance of cosmological principles to the pavement is indicated clearly by the final words of its inscription that refers to the "archetypal macrocosm." The relevance of the Arabic formula becomes clear when it is recalled that the use of the Latin term *arcanum* ("secret") in Medieval Europe was "certainly influenced directly by the Arabic word in question."[24] It was,

---

[23] *"Al-Arkān," Symbols of Sacred Science*, Hillsdale: Sophia Perennis, 2004.

[24] "The Cornerstone," *Symbols of Sacred Science*, op. cit.

after all, through the influence of Islam that the "arcane" sciences of the Pythagoreans came to be incorporated within Christendom during this period.

In his study, Richard Foster searches within Medieval Christendom for cosmological formulations comparable to the Sanctuary Pavement, and the closest example he offers is the rose window of Lausanne Cathedral. Significantly, Foster connects the development of this window to the School of Chartres.[25] In "The Labyrinth of the Age of Gold," I summarized evidence for this school being responsible for expressing the Apollonian tradition within the context of Christian and Islamic eschatology in the form of its labyrinth. [26] Foster muses on the close relationship between the labyrinth of Chartres and its rose window, but if he fails to understand the nature of the Apollonian tradition, he is even less able to consider the participation of the Islamic. This is so despite his admission that the central stone of the Sanctuary Pavement at Westminster is almost certainly

---

[25] Op. cit., pages 145-6.

[26] *Guardians of the Heart: Essays on Sacred Geography*, Temple of Justice Books, 2022. Part of this formulation concerns the significance of the number 19, which may be compared to the reckoning of some 19000 years according to the inscription within the "End of the World Pavement."

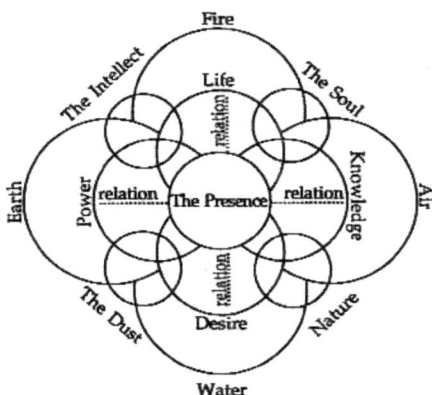

from Egypt, and that its glasswork betrays an Islamic origin.

If we consult the very authority who seems to be the source for the Islamic eschatology on display in Chartres, the Shaykh al-Akbar Muhyiddin Ibn `Arabi, we discover a cosmological diagram (above) worth comparing to the "End of the World Pavement:" According to the teachings of the Shaykh al-akbar (the "greatest master") who was also known as the "Son of Plato," the four elements may be envisioned as circles around a fifth circle; yet here there are other sets of four circles nearer to that center, and these may even be depicted at positions intermediate to the circles of the elements. [27] Here, then, is a solution to an aspect of the Westminster pavement's design that is a source of confusion for Foster. The art historian admits that his interpretation of the design is speculative, and somewhat inexplicably allows for more than one set of four elements. Still, his thoughts on the four circles nearest to the central stone in the pavement are not without merit, in particular his observation that the circle with its central point suggests the traditional symbol for the Sun while the circle containing the heptagon suggests a lunar aspect. In light of the above diagram, however, perhaps the solar circle is better associated with the Intellect, the active principle traditionally symbolized by the Sun. The other circles may then be related to the Soul, the Dust,[28] and Nature in turn.

In a series of articles on cosmological symbolism in which he makes reference to the *arkān*,[29] René Guénon insists that the central *rukn al-arkan* properly occupies a superior rank to the other four, a fact that is not easily understood

---

[27] This version of the Shaykh's diagram is from William C. Chittick, *The Self-Disclosure of God: Principles of Ibn al-`Arabi's Cosmology*, Albany: SUNY Press, 1997, page 230.

[28] The multi-rayed design within one of the circles especially suggests the multiplicity characterizing the cosmological Dust.

[29] "The Cornerstone," "*Lapsit Exillis*," and "*Al-Arkān*" in *Symbols of Sacred Science*, op. cit.

with diagrams restricted to a horizontal plane. Guénon therefore makes recourse to architectural symbolism that includes the vertical dimension in order to explain the identification of the *rukn al-arkan* with the "cornerstone." However, he explains that a symbolic "foundation stone" may be understood to belong to the same plane as the other *arkān* while having an axial relationship with the cornerstone. It is well known that the name Peter means "stone," and Guénon mentions the role of Saint Peter as a "foundation stone" in relation to Jesus Christ as cornerstone. It will further be recalled that Westminster Abbey is the Church of Saint Peter; but what is especially remarkable is that Guénon makes explicit reference to Westminster in the context of the mysterious stone, the *lapsit exillis* or Holy Grail, that operates, as it were, in the axial dimension:

> To return to the *lapsit exillis*, it must be pointed out that some have compared it to the *Lia Fail* or "stone of destiny" which was in fact also a "speaking stone" and furthermore may have been in a certain sense a "stone from heaven," since according to the Irish legend the *Tuatha de Danann* brought it with them from their first abode, to which is attributed a "celestial" character, or at least a "paradisal" one. This

> *Lia Fial* is known to have been
> the coronation stone [*pierre du
> sacre*] of Ireland's ancient kings,
> and it subsequently became that
> of the kings of England, having
> been brought by Edward I to
> Westminster Abbey according to
> the most widely held opinion;
> but what may seem strange is
> that this same stone, from
> another viewpoint, is identified
> with the one consecrated by
> Jacob at Bethel.[30]

Given the relationship of this "pillow" of Jacob
with the angelic ladder (*mi`raj*) he witnessed, the
identification of the Coronation Stone, or Stone of
Scone, with the stone of Bethel is perfectly
comprehensible, since it serves as a foundation
for superior influences.

As for the Sanctuary Pavement, it
provides a precise geometrical formulation of the
foundation stone positioned upon it, despite the
fact that it precedes the historical arrival of the
Coronation Stone itself. Enthroned upon the
Stone (see frontispiece) during the coronation,
the king is positioned over the five circles at the
center of the pavement; and given the celestial

---

[30] "*Lapsit Exillis,*" *Symbols of Sacred Science*, op. cit., page
281. Since 1996, the Coronation Stone has been held in
the spiritual center of Edinburgh.

portents attached to the accession of His Majesty King Charles III, it is worth recalling the literal meaning of the title "Pendragon:" "the 'chief of the five,' that is, the supreme king…situated at the center of the four subordinate kingdoms which correspond to the four cardinal points."[31] Obviously the British monarch unites the four lands of England, Wales, Scotland and Ireland most immediately. While the Coronation Stone is rectangular, and so in keeping with the encompassing square upon the pavement, Saint Edward's Crown is of course circular, so again we have the presence of symbols relating to Heaven and Earth, here joined through the "axial" body of the king. This crown is claimed to hold precisely 444 precious and semi-precious stones, and this number invites an important observation. 444 is 4 times 111; and while 4 has just been specified as the number of subordinate kingdoms, I have often insisted on the importance of 111 in Islamic esoterism, and I have even had occasion to note its presence in the British national epic *The Lord of the Rings*.[32] According to gematria, 111 is the number of the name of the axial letter *alif* as well as the number of the title *qutb* ("pole" or "axis") for the highest

---

[31] "The Wild Boar and the Bear," *Symbols of Sacred Science*, op. cit., page 163.

[32] *Alchemy in Middle-earth: The Significance of J.R.R. Tolkien's The Lord of the Rings*, Temple of Justice Books, 2003, page 85.

Cypher of HM The King

rank of spiritual authority. This number is moreover present in the cypher of His Majesty King Charles III, since 3 in Roman numerals is indistinguishable from 111.

Finally there is the significance of the date chosen for the coronation, 6 May.[33] Again, while 23 April is the day of England's patron Saint George, this date on the Julian calendar corresponds to 6 May on the modern Gregorian. In the lands of the Ottoman Empire, where Christians followed the Julian calendar, Muslims

---

[33] There is a further coincidence to be noted, since this date of the 5th month brings together the number 5 and 6 that were associated above with the relationship of Earth and Heaven. For that matter, the Islamic or Hijri date of the coronation belongs to the year 1444, so here again the number 444 is present.

and Christians respected 6 May as the spring festival of Hidrellez, the name of which is a conjunction of the names of Khidr, or Saint George, and of Elias, or Elijah. Now, according to the teachings of Islamic esoterism, these ever-living prophets belong to a rank of four that also includes Jesus, as well as Idris in his solar abode who is called the *qutb*.[34] These four are invested with supreme authority over all spiritual and worldly affairs, and with a Christian king's crown of 444 stones, the ceremony on Hidrellez should be understood to be under the benediction of all four chiefs of the saintly hierarchy. Despite the role played by the Archbishop of Canterbury, his is not the supreme authority, and even Saint Edward whose crown he presumes to bestow did not follow the Church of England.

Much to the irritation of the Archbishop, the future king long ago made clear his intention to serve in "defending faith itself" rather than the Church of England only,[35] and it is expected that his coronation ceremony will be the most ecumenical in Britain's history. In defining his

---

[34] Just as Idris occupies a position at once both solar and axial, Apollo has both solar and polar attributes, the latter by virtue of his being Hyperborean; in this connection it may be recalled that his periodic visit to the Hyperboreans is sometimes calculated as occurring every 19 years.

[35] Cf. *Alchemy in Middle-earth*, op. cit., pages 77 and 94.

incomparable role in that history, he has used the unofficial title "Defender of Nature;" and given the importance of Nature in Islamic cosmology, as we have seen, his defense of Islam is consistent with his defense of nature's importance. His Majesty has already presented a manifesto that is essentially Pythagorean,[36] and his reign as a philosopher king in the Platonic sense has long been anticipated. Now the arcane is on display for the coronation of His Majesty King Charles III in Westminster, where "end of the Prime Mover" might better be translated "purpose of the *qutb*;" and with this saintly renewal of ancient tradition there is hope that, in the words of Virgil, "the iron race shall begin to cease, and the golden to arise over all the world."

---

[36] This manifesto is the book *Harmony: A New Way of Looking at the World*; see *Sacred Geography and the Paths of the Sun*, pages 115-6.

On HRH Prince Philip and Hercules

The funeral of HRH Prince Philip has attracted the world's attention once again to Windsor and its chapel of Saint George. The occasion concerns, however, not only one but rather two of the Spiritual Centers of Britain because of the departed Prince's distinction as the Duke of Edinburgh, a rarely used title that was revived especially for him. Born as heir to the kingdoms of Denmark and Greece, HRH Prince Philip relinquished these claims for a most remarkable life of service that spanned a full century, and no doubt his memory warrants much better treatment than may be offered here, but the convergence of Windsor and Edinburgh is but one of many aspects of his funeral that should not be overlooked. The Seven Spiritual Centers of Britain is a subject addressed in *Sacred Geography and the Paths of the Sun,* and the reader is directed there for more explanation, in addition concerning the identity of Saint George as al-Khidr, the Green Man,[37] and so as one of the chiefs of the living spiritual hierarchy. Among the other locations figuring in that work, the island of Corfu proved to be of particular relevance, and so it is worth mentioning again that Corfu was the birthplace of HRH Prince Philip.

In this work, the island of Corfu is introduced as the location of one of the seven tombs of the dragon slayer Sari Saltik. In quoting from the account of Alexandre Degrand, what was not mentioned is that according to the lore of the Albanian Bektashi dervishes, the dragon that was slain by the saint was specifically a "kuçedra," that is, a hydra.[38] This detail demands that this hagiography be compared to the heroic cycle of Hercules that is so well known in the region, since the slaying of a hydra constituted

---

[37] The identification of Saint George with al-Khidr was confirmed by HRH The Prince of Wales in his speech at the memorial of HM King Hussein of Jordan in 1999.
[38] While the nature of this hydra was, of course, malevolent, it is important to recall that the benevolent aspect of the symbolism of the dragon is nonetheless present. Following the slaying of the seven-headed hydra, Sari Saltik takes up residence in the dragon's cave, thereby becoming a saintly dragon himself; and what is more, his ultimate association with seven tombs is clearly related to the seven heads of the dragon he replaced.

the second of the 12 Labors of the ancient hero.
As if to remove any doubt as to the relevance of
this comparison, Degrand includes another
curious detail, that the true identity of the dragon
slayer is confirmed by the rescued princess' gift
of three apples. The attaining of the Golden
Apples of the Hesperides who were the
daughters of Atlas was, of course, the
penultimate of Hercules' Labors, and indicates
perhaps more than any other of the Labors the
solar nature of the hero. Clearly the solar aspect
of this legend has a particular significance in the
context of the "paths of the Sun," but what
concerns us here is that the coat of arms of HRH
Prince Philip includes so conspicuously the
figure of Hercules:

Here the heraldic Hercules should not be confused with the Wild Man, since the latter is properly covered in hair, and in this example it is rather the pelt of the Nemean Lion that covers the solar hero's nakedness and relates to the first of his Labors. Along with his mythological importance, however, there is another dimension to Hercules' legacy that must not be overlooked. The philosopher Diogenes the Cynic wrote a dialogue entitled "Hercules," at least according to Diogenes Laertius; and while the dialogue is not extant, the latter observed that Diogenes the Cynic "maintained that his life was of the same stamp as that of Hercules." According to Dio Chrysostom, Diogenes explained that Hercules "thought his duty to consist no less in a magnanimous contest with the vanities of popular opinion." This description, of course, eminently characterizes the example of HRH Prince Philip, whose oft-recalled controversial statements clashed with the expectations of popular opinion. No doubt, in the words of HRH Prince Charles who for a time succeeded his father as the Duke of Edinburgh, Prince Philip "didn't suffer fools gladly."

It will be recalled that the naming of Windsor and Edinburgh among the Seven Spiritual Centers of Britain belongs to the teachings of Shaykh Nazim al-Haqqani. In the present context, it is very remarkable indeed that the first lesson offered by the great master from what he identified as the "Moonlight Academy" of Edinburgh concerned counsel given to Alexander the Great by none other than Diogenes the Cynic. If it is preferred that a prince should be compared rather with Alexander the Great than with Diogenes, remember that HRH Prince Philip had abandoned his inherited pretensions. Obviously Philip is the namesake of Alexander's father, yet here, as in the example of Diogenes with Alexander, we may presume it has been at least in part due to a father's counsels that his eldest son has been in his life so dedicated to truth. Upon the death of Hercules, the solar hero was welcomed into the divine company of Olympus; and with the funeral of Philip the Garter knight in Saint George's Chapel, we hope that his long life of service has led to him being welcomed into a most holy company indeed.

The Wedding of the Duke and Duchess of Sussex[39]

Before his passing, the great saint Shaykh Nazim al-Haqqani Naqshbandi gave a remarkable teaching in which he mentions seven centers of spirituality in Great Britain, concerning which I have already had occasion to comment. His identification of some of these locations followed his personal reflections on the excellence of the House of Windsor, and included references to the abdication of Edward VIII. Now, if nothing else, it is remarkable that so many on both sides of the Atlantic – and well beyond – should be so focused recently on events appearing in one of the locations that he did identify, Windsor, of which the house is the namesake.

---

[39] Most of this essay appeared online in 2018 as "Some Observations on the Royal Wedding at Windsor."

The events on display, of course, were those of a royal wedding ceremony. Now, the mixed race of the American bride has caused much excitement, and was reflected not too subtly in the choice of speakers and performers at the ceremony. Before commenting on some of the more significant elements of the wedding at Windsor, I would like to quote from some related comments I made some years ago,[40] on matters that quite unexpectedly have found a renewed relevance:

> During the political campaign of Barack Hussein Obama, and no doubt contributing to its success, the President-elect was dubbed an adopted "son of Camelot," that is, of the Kennedy legacy. When this reference is traced beyond its residual meaning in American politics to its Medieval Arthurian source, Obama's rise to the world stage assumes a greater significance than even his supporters imagine.
>
> Clearly Obama's most distinctive mark is his mixed

---

[40] I was not alone in making these observations. In particular, the comments of Pir Zia Khan at the time rendered my comments somewhat unnecessary.

parentage: black and white…Since his racial composition is celebrated as representative of the American experience, it could be offered that the very symbol of the United States, the bald eagle, is properly a "piebald" eagle, that is, black and white. Now, there is at the core of Arthurian literature a "piebald" figure whose parentage is similarly mixed, and he is Feirefiz in Wolfram von Eschenbach's *Parzival*.

The great ruler Feirefiz too becomes an "adopted son" of Arthur's court. Even though it is the mother of Feirefiz who is black, and so unlike the example of Obama, it is at least curious that the father of Feirefiz served the Muslim "Baruch," when Obama's father gave his son the Arabic form of the same name! Of course, the ease with which America with its "Indians" may be confounded with Feirefiz' India should not be overlooked. When Feirefiz' journey in search of his patrimony brings him to

47

> Britain, he discovers his half-brother Parzival of Wales, and their reconciliation is inextricably bound to the attainment of the Grail quest.

Despite the absence of the Obama family from the wedding at Windsor – in keeping with the decision not to invite politicians - it must be admitted that the family became noticeably close with the House of Windsor during the Obama presidency, and perhaps most of all with Prince Harry, who personally conducted a broadcast interview with Obama following his terms in office. In any case, quite beyond the personal involvement of Obama with the symbolism surrounding him, the wedding of Prince Harry to an American of mixed race is a kind of fulfillment of the matters described above, especially since the attainment of the black and white figure includes a marriage into the Grail Family. That being said, the presence at the ceremony of an Archbishop of the Coptic Church, that is, of Egypt, suggests that the meanings on display at Windsor were intended to resonate further afield.

The key to this resonance is to be found in the choice of scripture for the ceremony, namely the *Song of Solomon*. Of course, this choice would seem to be appropriate for any wedding, given its themes of love, but the bride at Windsor may especially be seen to exemplify the "black" and "beautiful" Shulamite of the *Song*. The identity of the Shulamite's beloved is traditionally understood to be Solomon[41] of the line of David, peace be upon them, and so it is suggestive that David is mentioned in the ceremony as another name of the prince. Legend assumes the mysterious Shulamite bride to be none other than the one with whom Solomon is traditionally paired, the black Queen of Sheba, who travels from afar to the Temple; and for Josephus at least, the Queen of Sheba was also the Queen of Egypt. Beyond the Egyptian context of the archbishop's presence, the arrival of the bride at the chapel – with her youthful attendants and no one to "give her away" - certainly recalls the independent lady of power who travels from afar. Perhaps most explicitly of all, the chosen setting supports the Solomonic theme, since the checkered black and white floor of the chapel at Windsor is a Masonic motif referring to the Temple of Solomon in Jerusalem, and is reinforced by the black or white dress of the participants.[42]

More generally, the Queen of Sheba is ruler of the south, and while the prince's bride is American, she has been granted by HM The Queen a title relating to the south of England or

---

[41] The meanings of "Solomon" and "Shulamite" both relate to "peace."

[42] It need hardly be pointed out that the symbolism here is comparable to the balance of yin and yang in the Chinese tradition.

Sussex. More specifically, the American bride has displayed her Californian identity by including that state's flower alongside floral emblems of each of the Commonwealth of Nations in her veil.[43] Yet here again is a strange confirmation of her embodiment of the bride from the *Song of Solomon*, since California is originally associated in chivalric literature with a black and independent queen named Califia (from the Arabic *khalifah*) who is but another formulation of the Queen of Sheba.[44] Of course, the "royalty" with which the bride had been associating in California was that of Hollywood, and indeed some of the guests at the wedding belong to that company; however, this illusory royalty has been replaced for her by true royalty, as the former actress is expected to perform a new role in earnest, just as the Queen of Sheba in the *Qur'an* is challenged to perceive the truth when she joins the Prophet Sulaiman in the Temple.[45]

---

[43] It may seem strange to represent California alongside the Commonwealth of Nations, unless we consider that Sir Francis Drake is presumed to have claimed Northern California as part of New Albion for Elizabeth I in 1579.

[44] Note that the mother of Feirefiz was also compared to the Queen of Sheba in Helen Adolf's "New Light on Oriental Sources for Wolfram's *Parzival* and other Grail Romances" (*PMLA*, volume 62, number 2, Cambridge: Cambridge University Press, June 1947).

[45] XXVII, 42-4

According to the especially rich esoteric interpretation of the *Song of Solomon*, the Shulamite bride is the embodiment of the Shekhinah, the feminine "Divine Peace" as well as the power of manifesting that Peace. In the former sense, the Shekhinah is associated with light; and the bride's approach down the aisle of the Windsor chapel was to the tune of Handel's "Eternal Source of Light Divine" with its chorus calling for "lasting peace on earth." The power of the Shekhinah is in turn associated with fire; so special attention should be given to the commentary of the Episcopal bishop in the ceremony, concerning the fire that transcends the fire of technology and that might establish a new world. Since the Shekhinah is in a sense the synthesis of the ten *sephirot* of the Tree of Life, it is worth observing further that the number of youthful attendants accompanying the bride to the Windsor chapel was ten. Even more remarkably, the woman's name in Lurian Kabbalah associated with the Shekhinah in exile is none other than Rachel, that is, the first name by which the bride was called in the ceremony. [46]

According to René Guénon, the scriptural references for the Shekhinah are

---

[46] The Shekhinah (*Sakinah* in Arabic) is sometimes described in Islamic sources as "a basin of gold in which the hearts of the prophets were washed" (*The History of al-Tabari* volume III), and this recalls the Grail itself.

especially concerned with the establishment of spiritual centers. Considering Shaykh Nazim al-Haqqani Naqshbandi's indication of Windsor as a spiritual center in England, the enacting or "conjuration" of the *Song of Solomon* with this royal marriage is significant indeed, since the *Song* concerns nothing less than the restoration of cosmic harmony. In a profound way, the wedding demonstrates the promise of a blessed reconciliation between Britain and America.

✡

Unfortunately, the "alchemical conjunction" shown to the world from the spiritual center of Windsor stands in stark contrast to the disharmony that has come to characterize the wedding couple's relationship with the rest of the royal family. Edward VIII was mentioned at the outset of the article, and his decision to abdicate the throne in order to marry an American as the Duke of Windsor would seem to provide a kind of precedent for a rupture caused by a royal marriage. However, the nationality of the former king's bride had little to do with her unsuitability to serve as Queen Consort; rather it was the fact that she was twice a divorcée. While Duchess Meghan is likewise a divorcée, she is not a candidate for Queen Consort.

Here it is worth emphasizing the

remarkable fact that the wives of both sons of HM King Charles III are from common backgrounds, and this would seem to be a legacy of their mother Diana who was famously hailed as the "People's Princess." However, Princess Diana's background was far from common, and it is rather the exemplary Princess Katherine who is truly a princess "of the people,"[47] especially since becoming the first Princess of Wales after Diana chose to abandon the title.[48] Somewhat disconcertingly, considering Princess Diana's tragic fate, the Sussexes have insisted on drawing comparisons with her example in attempting to justify their decision to no longer serve as working royals.

Before refusing the roles offered to them, the Duke and Duchess welcomed their first child on 6 May 2019, and 6 May is the same day of honor associated with Saint George that would be chosen for the coronation of HM The King. This recalls the central importance of Saint

---

[47] This recalls a saying in the Islamic tradition attributed to `Ali, the King of Men (*Shah-i mardan*): "Nobility is not from the bones of ancestors but from one's character."

[48] No less exemplary is HRH Prince William, who is expected now to follow his father in fulfilling the heraldic motto of the Prince of Wales, *Ich dien* ("I serve"). Their Royal Highnesses were appointed Prince and Princess of Wales by HM The King without fanfare. Like his father, Prince William is also named Arthur.

George at Windsor, for the chapel where they were married is properly the headquarters of the world's most distinguished order of chivalry, the Order of the Garter, that is dedicated to Saint George.

Even the eventual relocation of the Sussexes to California resonates with the intrinsic themes of their wedding. The Duchess' specific bond with California was after all displayed upon her veil, and their "exile," though self-imposed, recalls the exile of the Shekhinah. Duchess Meghan was specifically compared above with Queen Califia, yet in Spanish romance this Queen of California has a clearly ambivalent aspect, alternatively opposing and supporting Christian chivalry. In this regard the legendary island of California is analogous to the island of Avalon in Arthurian romance. Both islands belong to an all-female company, and the Queen of Avalon is Morgan le Fay, who "despite her depiction as an evil sorceress throughout Arthurian legend, she first plays a perfectly benevolent role as caretaker to the wounded King

The Duchess' Royal Monogram

Arthur."[49] Without dwelling on the coincidence, and despite no etymological link between the two, it may be admitted that the name of the Californian Duchess is even similar to the name Morgan.

Yet modern California is very far from Avalon, and there is an undeniably sinister aspect to the couple's seeming selfishness. Leaving aside cynical observations on the "bewitching" of a prince, it is still better to hope that since the benevolence of Morgan le Fay is expressed through her caretaking of wounded royalty, the much-publicized psychological wounds that have plagued Prince Harry will somehow be healed through the peculiarities of his destiny. The reconciliation of Britain and America will just have to wait;[50] but as we have seen with the long-anticipated crowning of the new king, it is only a matter of time.

---

[49] *The Nine Sisters and the Caretakers of California, Paths of the Western Sun* volume II, forthcoming. However, it should be noted that the couple have settled in a place far removed from the Elizabethan New Albion; this area of California instead belonged to Britain's principal rival, the Spanish Empire.

[50] In order for an even greater reconciliation between Britain and America to be accomplished, it should not be overlooked that as a defender of nature and tradition, His Majesty is a champion of Native America; he is known among the Blackfeet as Red Crow.

www.ingramcontent.com/pod-product-compliance
Lightning Source LLC
Chambersburg PA
CBHW042338040426
42447CB00017B/3470